Color By Number
Butterflies

A FEW SINCERE WORDS FOR YOU

We appreciate you picking our coloring book amongst so many others. Your feedback is the highest compliment and source of motivation we could have acquired although we are aware that there are brilliant authors, who have written and released other excellent books.

BEFORE YOU GO

We hope you love our books and would genuinely appreciate it if you could share the sections you colored on social networks with the hashtags: #southernlotus #southernlotuscoloringbook #southernlotuscoloring

In addition, we are eager to read your Amazon reviews. We value all constructive comments, and we'll take them into careful consideration as we work to enhance both our books and our community.

Please feel free to reach out to us if you have any questions.
coloring@southernlotus.com

Visit our social media pages and follow us by using the code below:

This book belongs to

....

Test color page

1
White
#ffffff

2
Light Yellow
#fffdac

3
Yellow
#fff300

4
Dark Yellow
#dbb53a

5
Light Orange
#ffbf4f

6
Orange
#ff8b00

7
Dark Orange
#de5316

8
Light Pink
#ffa9cd

9
Pink
#cc819d

10
Dark Pink
#aa0243

11
Light Red
#ff6c6e

12
Red
#f61d20

13
Dark Red
#a41e25

14
Light Green
#ccff01

15
Green
#89a801

16
Dark Green
#658100

17
Cyan
#07b2b1

18
Light Blue
#acccff

19
Blue
#294cd1

20
Dark Blue
#2d3988

21
Light Purple
#aa37c9

22
Purple
#670080

23
Dark Purple
#450055

24
Light Brown
#905b25

25
Brown
#664019

26
Dark Brown
#3d2c12

27
Light Gray
#bebebe

28
Gray
#838383

29
Dark Gray
#474747

30
Black
#000000

Test color page

1
White
#ffffff

2
Light Yellow
#fffdac

3
Yellow
#fff300

4
Dark Yellow
#dbb53a

5
Light Orange
#ffbf4f

6
Orange
#ff8b00

7
Dark Orange
#de5316

8
Light Pink
#ffa9cd

9
Pink
#cc819d

10
Dark Pink
#aa0243

11
Light Red
#ff6c6e

12
Red
#f61d20

13
Dark Red
#a41e25

14
Light Green
#ccff01

15
Green
#89a801

16
Dark Green
#658100

17
Cyan
#07b2b1

18
Light Blue
#acccff

19
Blue
#294cd1

20
Dark Blue
#2d3988

21
Light Purple
#aa37c9

22
Purple
#670080

23
Dark Purple
#450055

24
Light Brown
#905b25

25
Brown
#664019

26
Dark Brown
#3d2c12

27
Light Gray
#bebebe

28
Gray
#838383

29
Dark Gray
#474747

30
Black
#000000

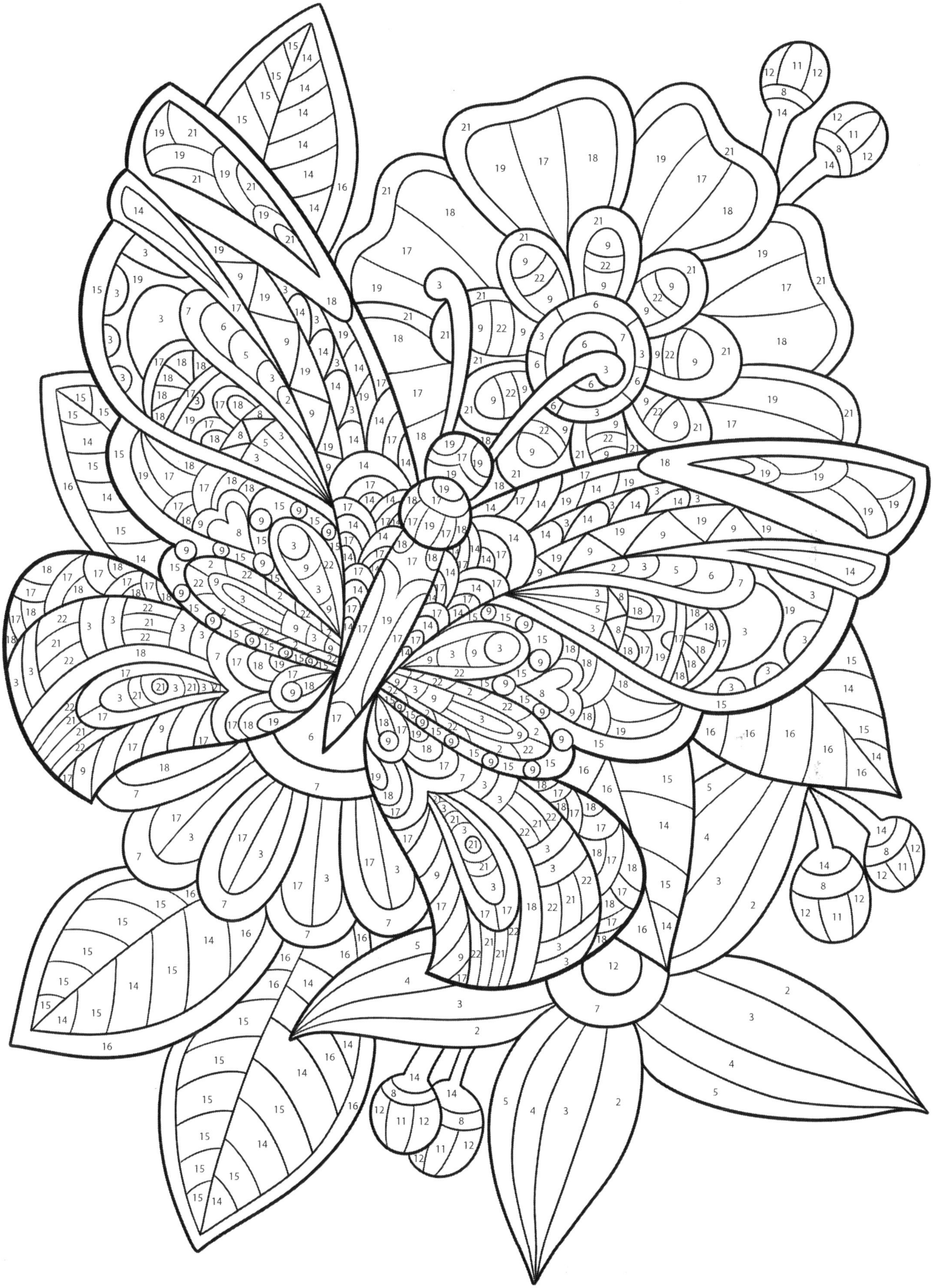

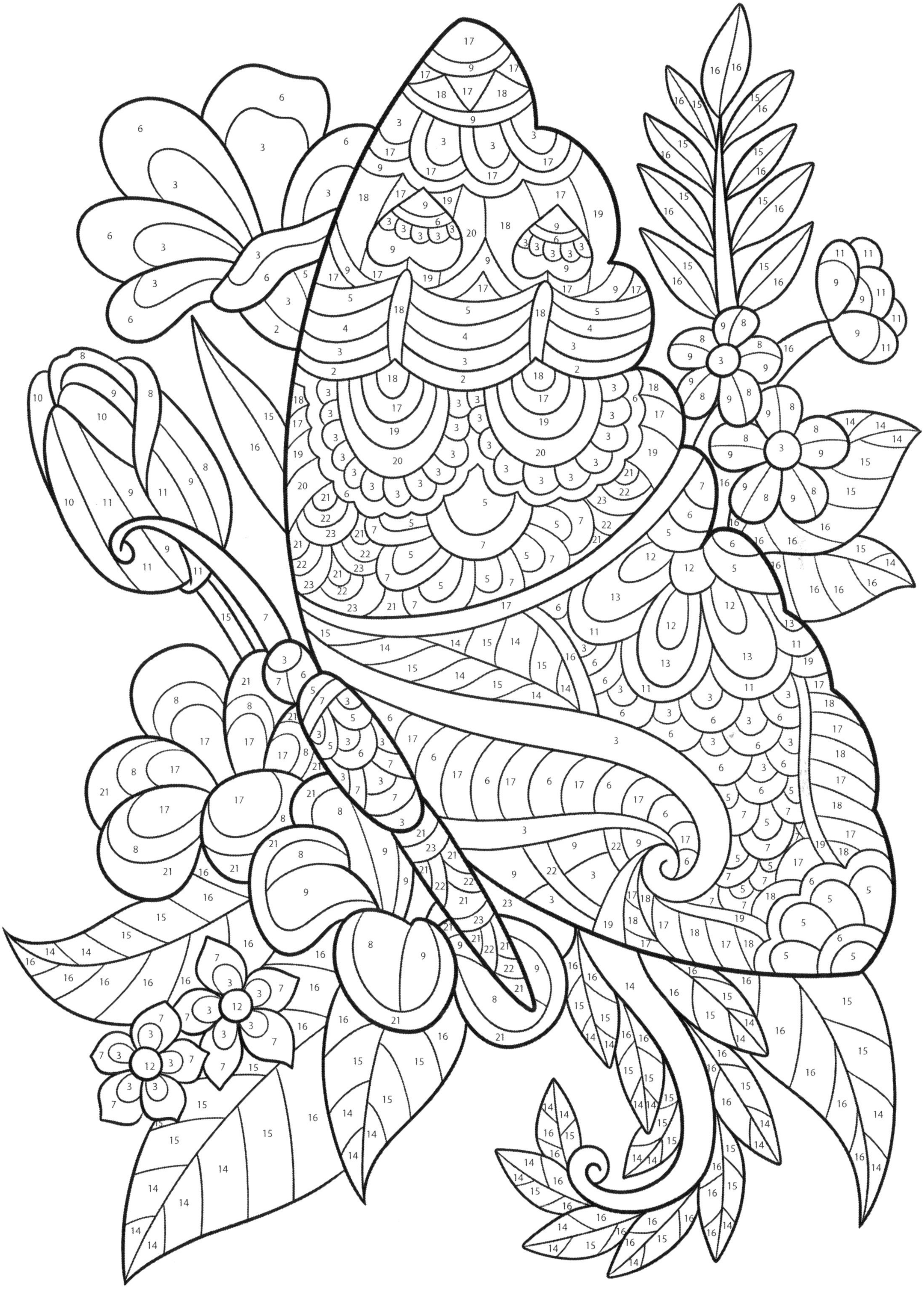

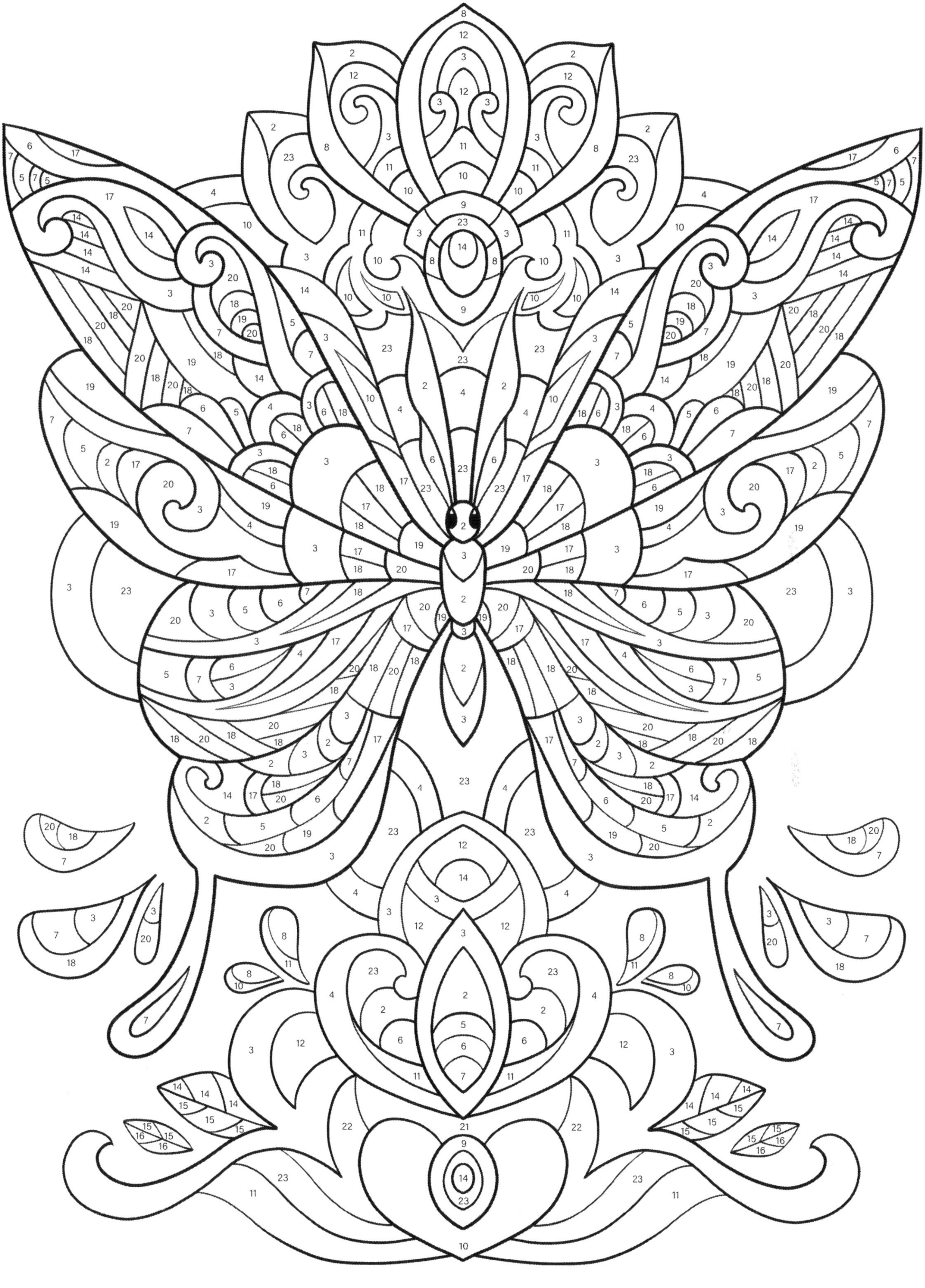

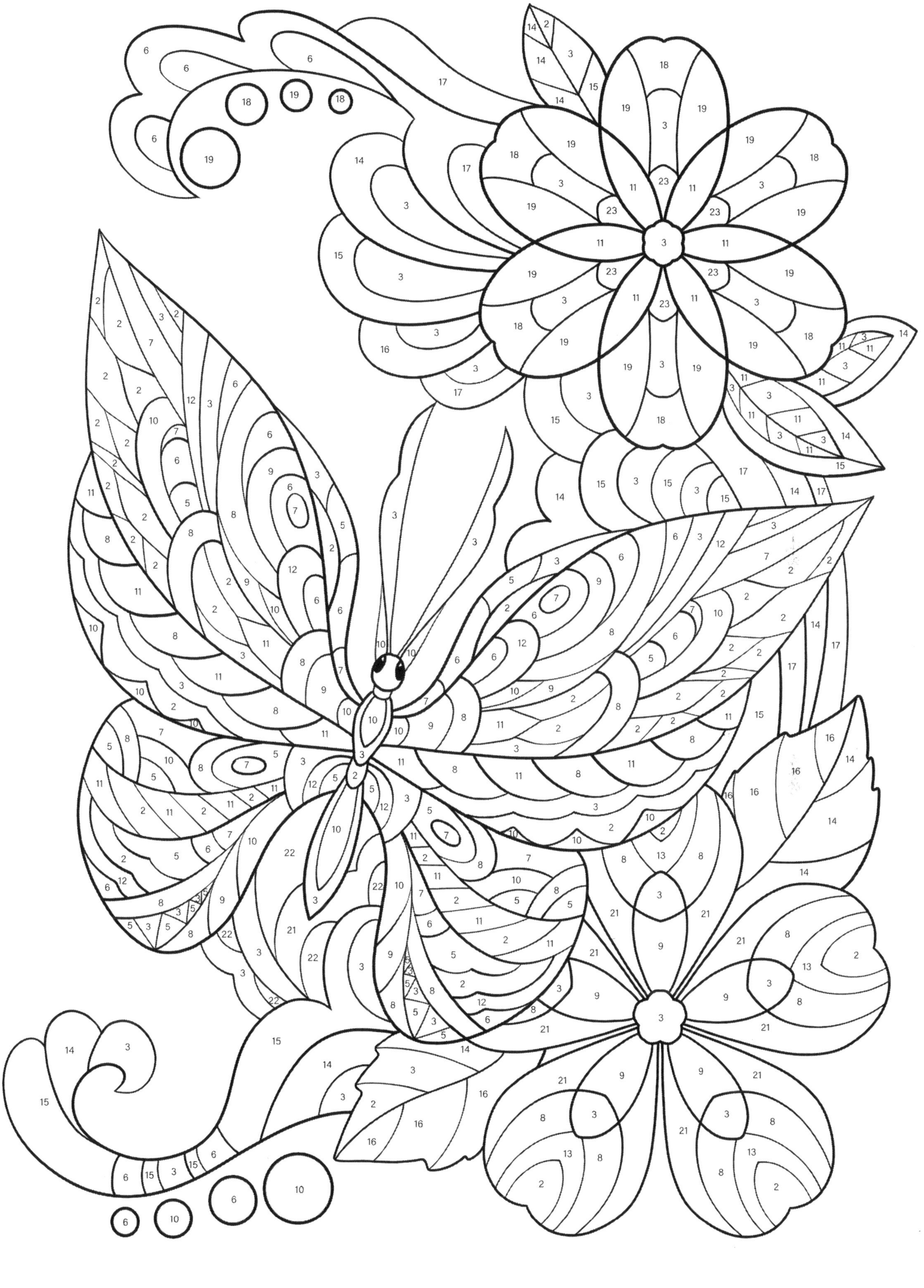

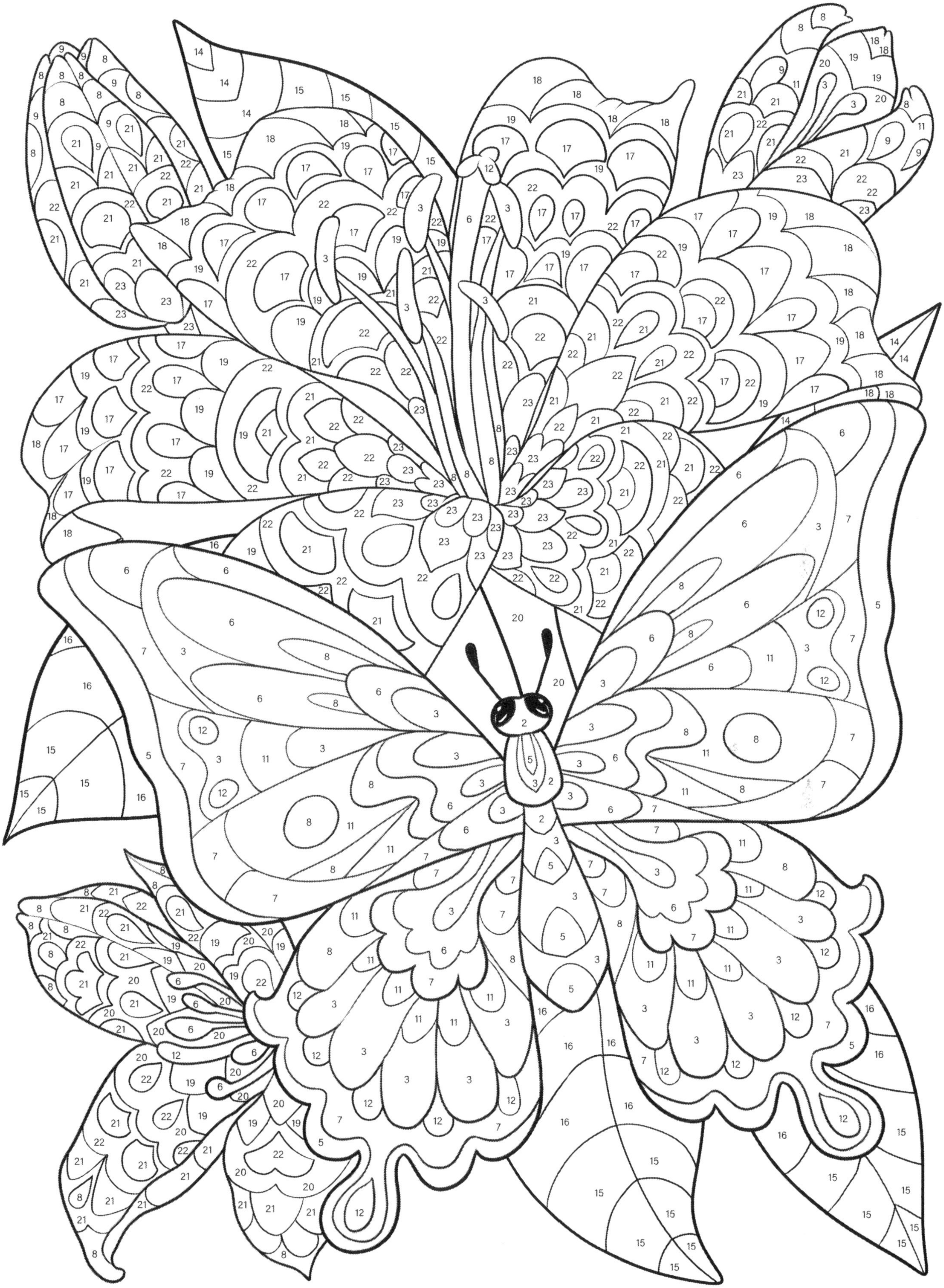

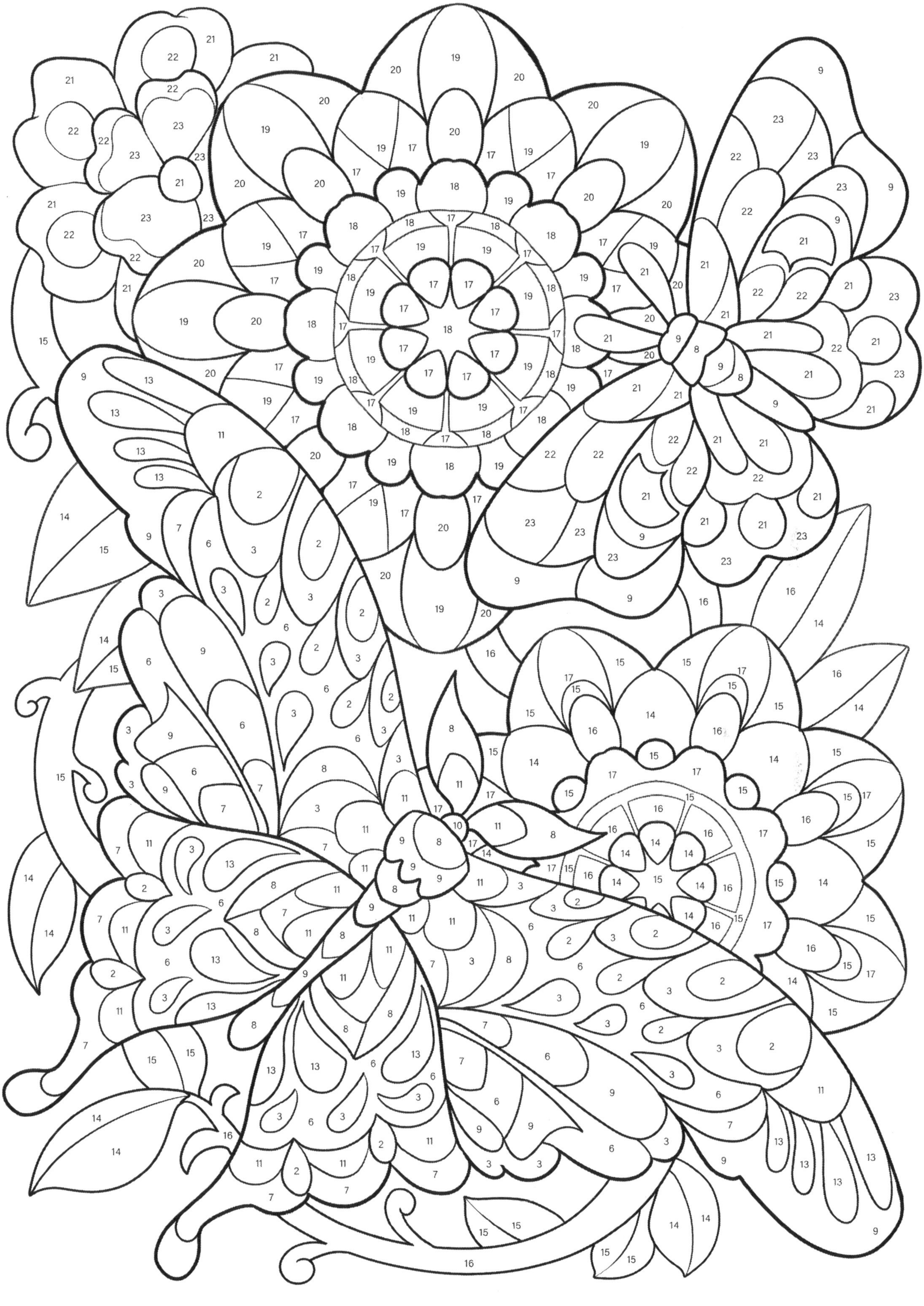

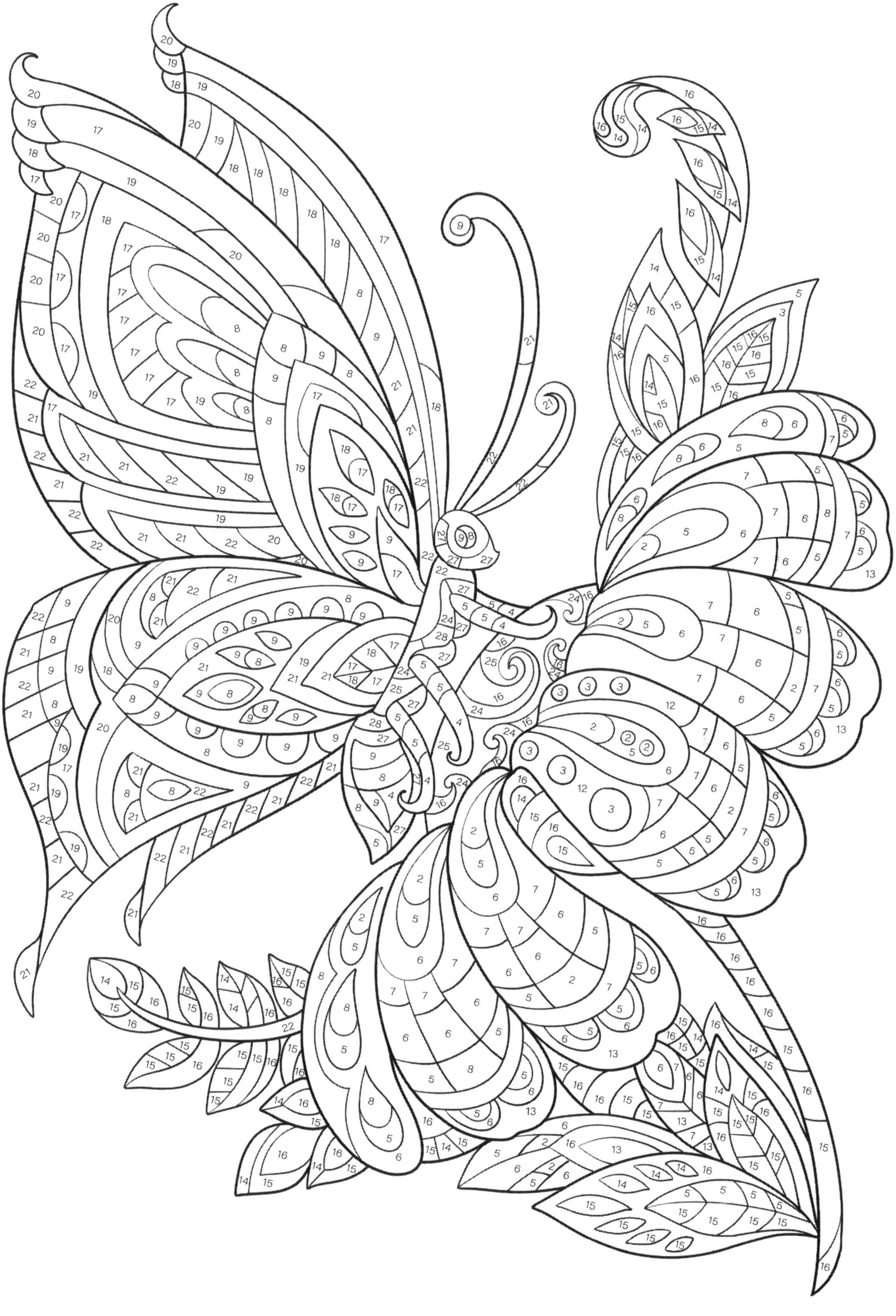

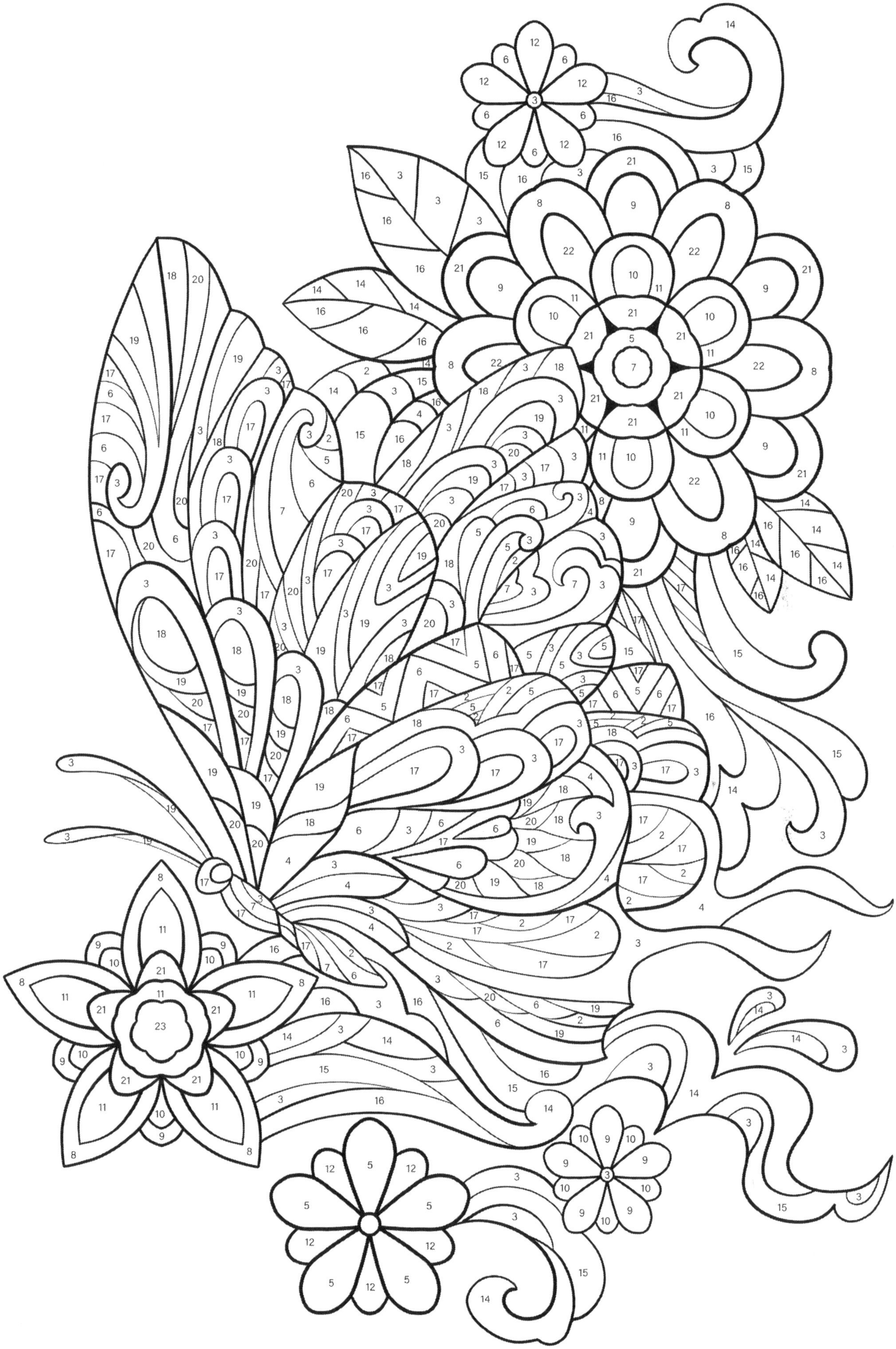

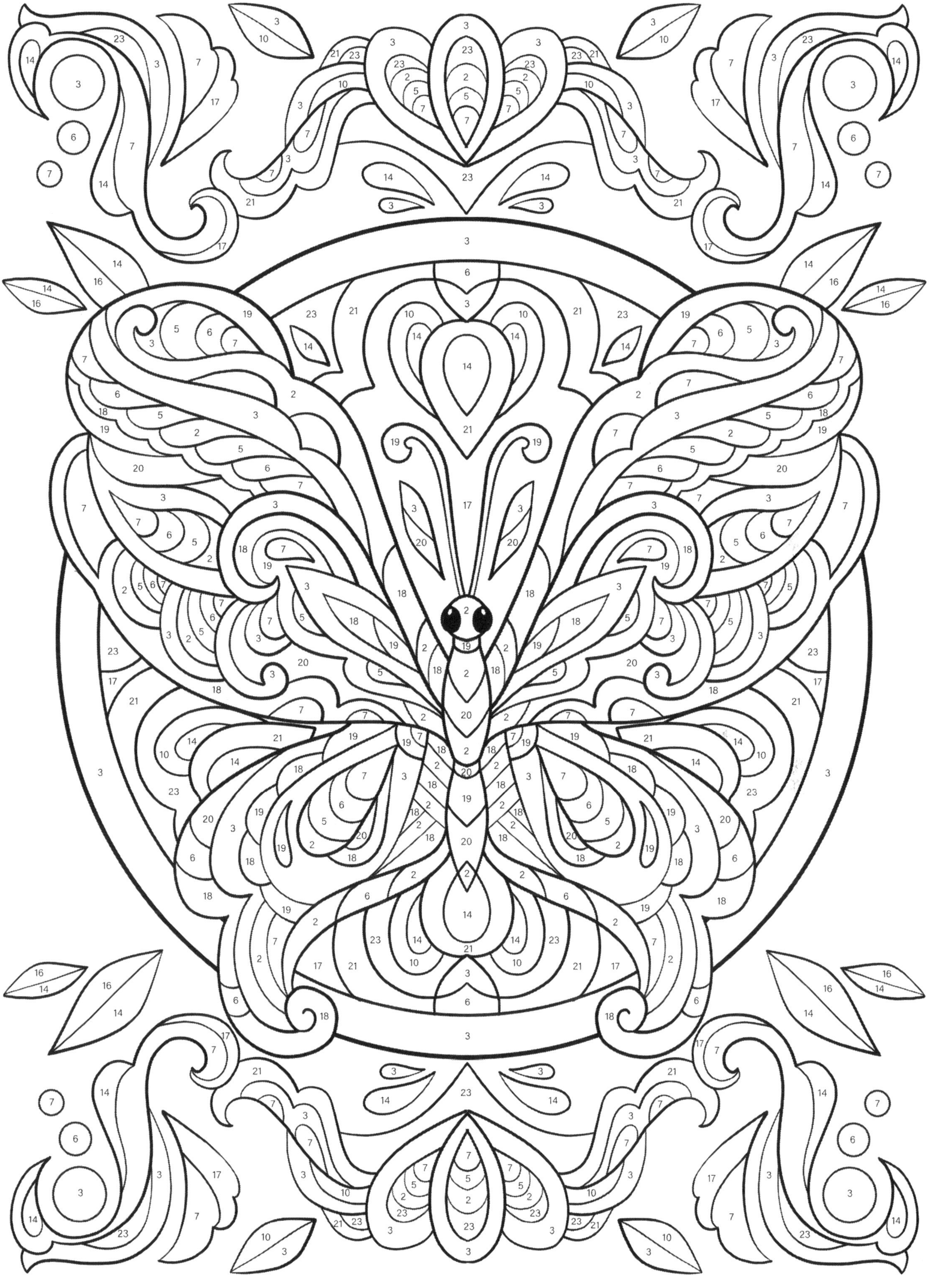

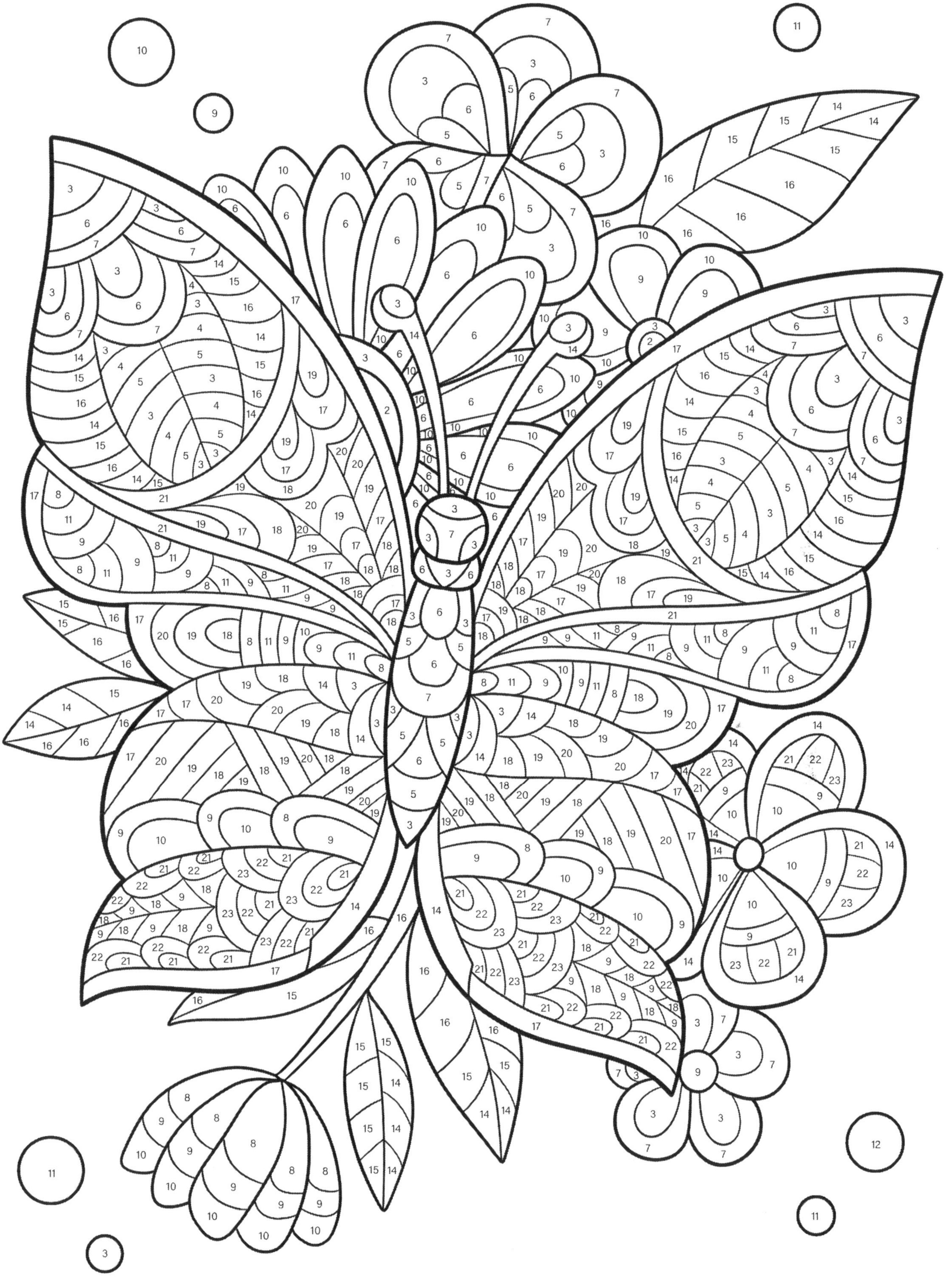

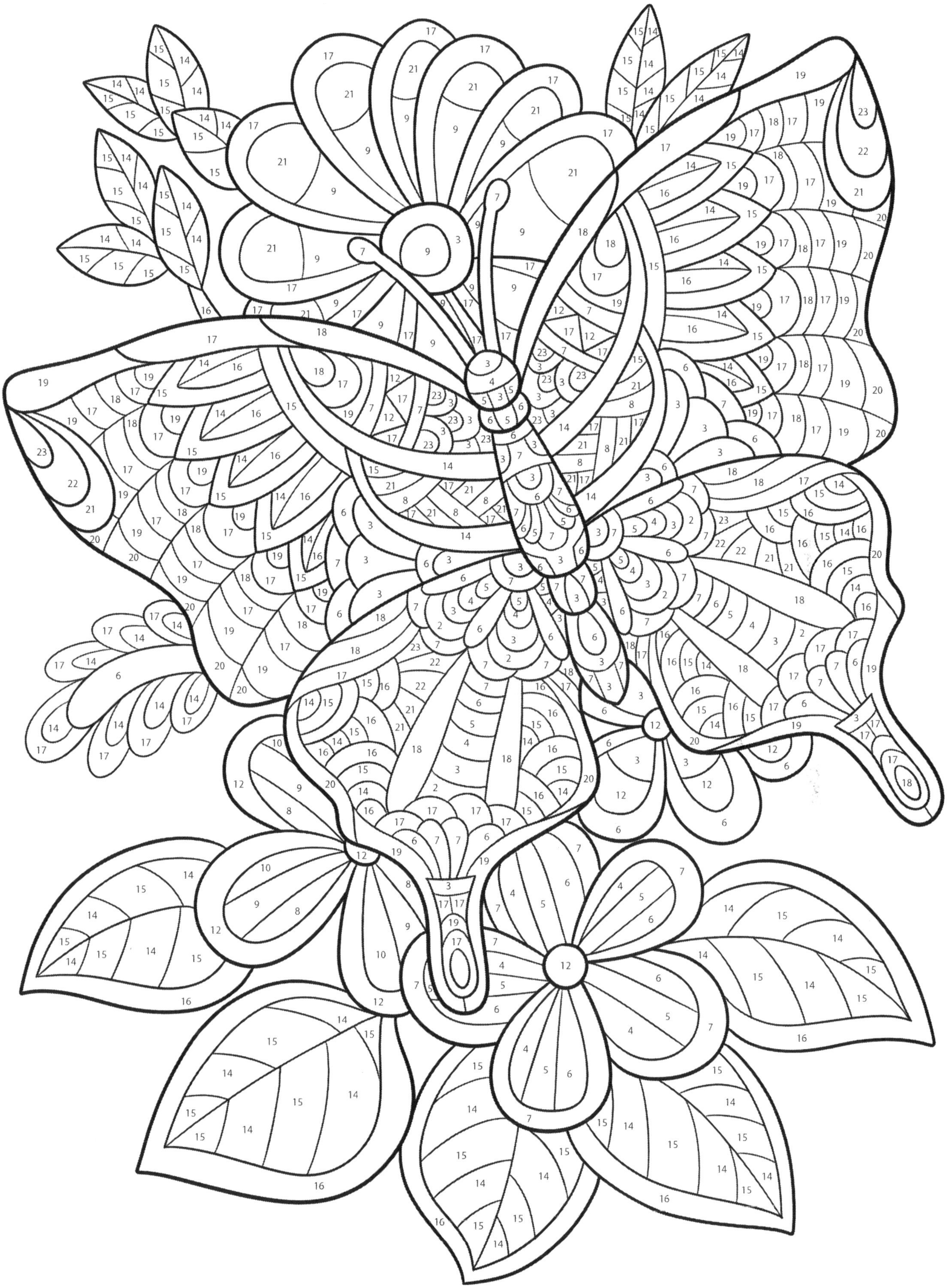

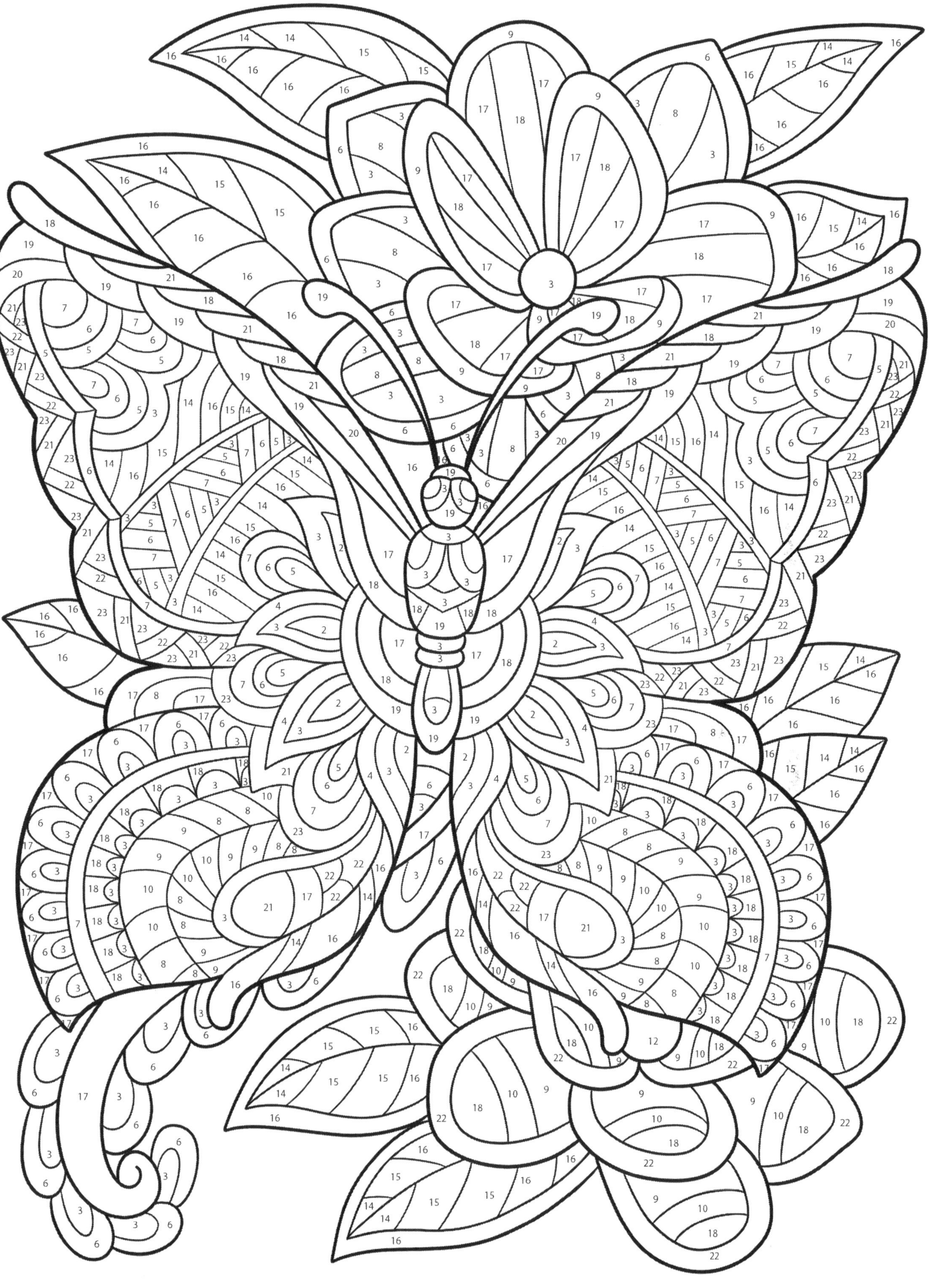

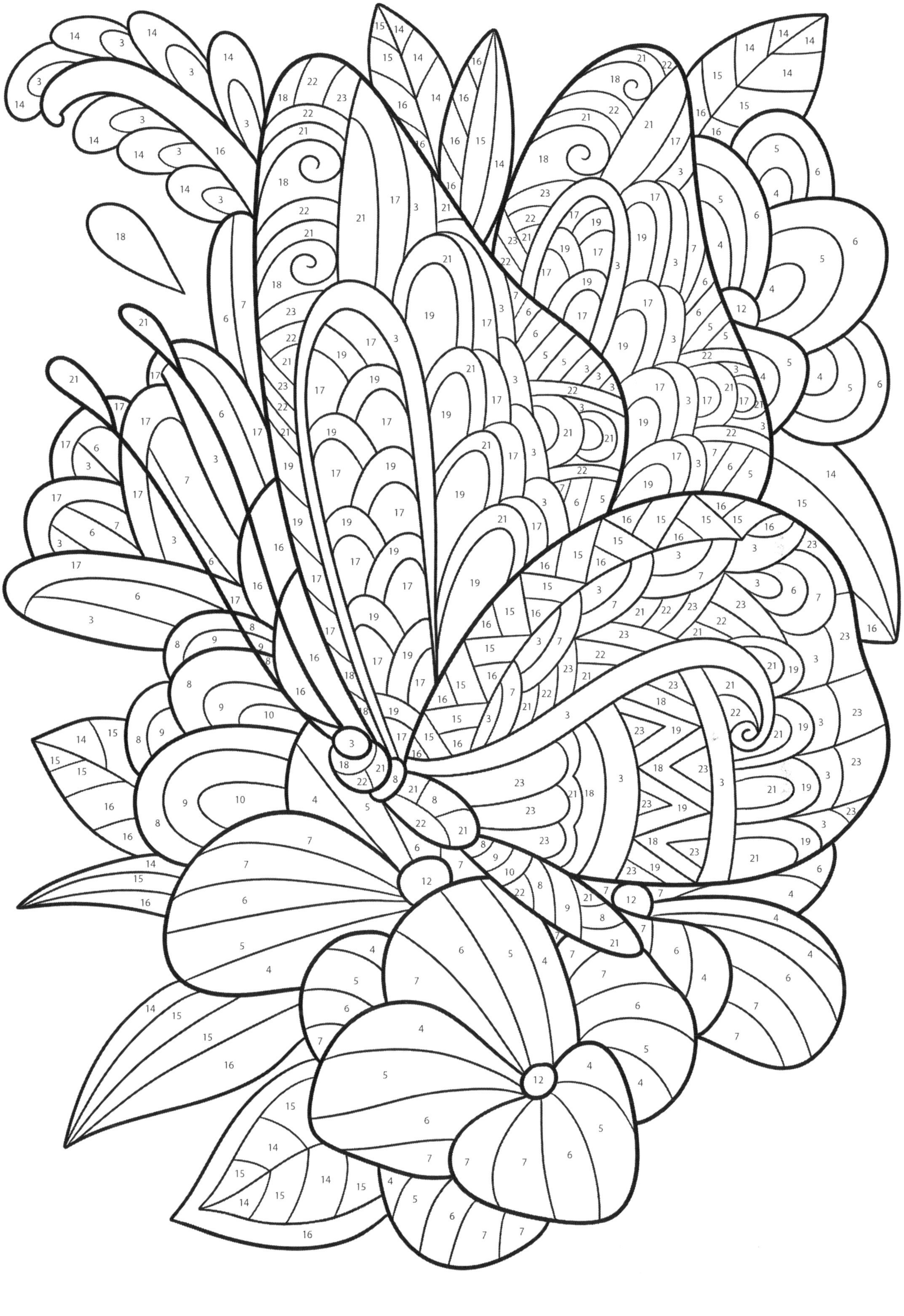

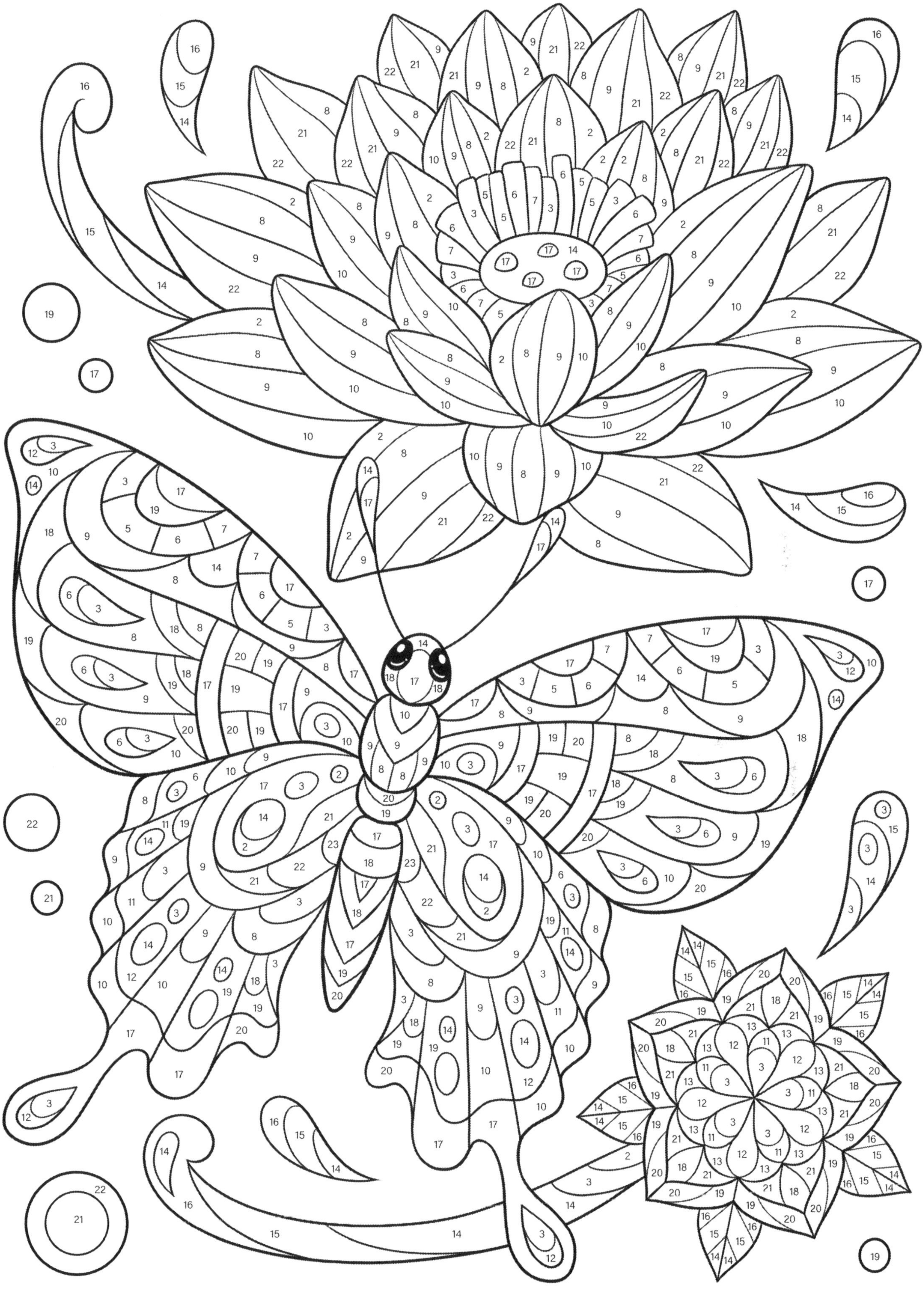

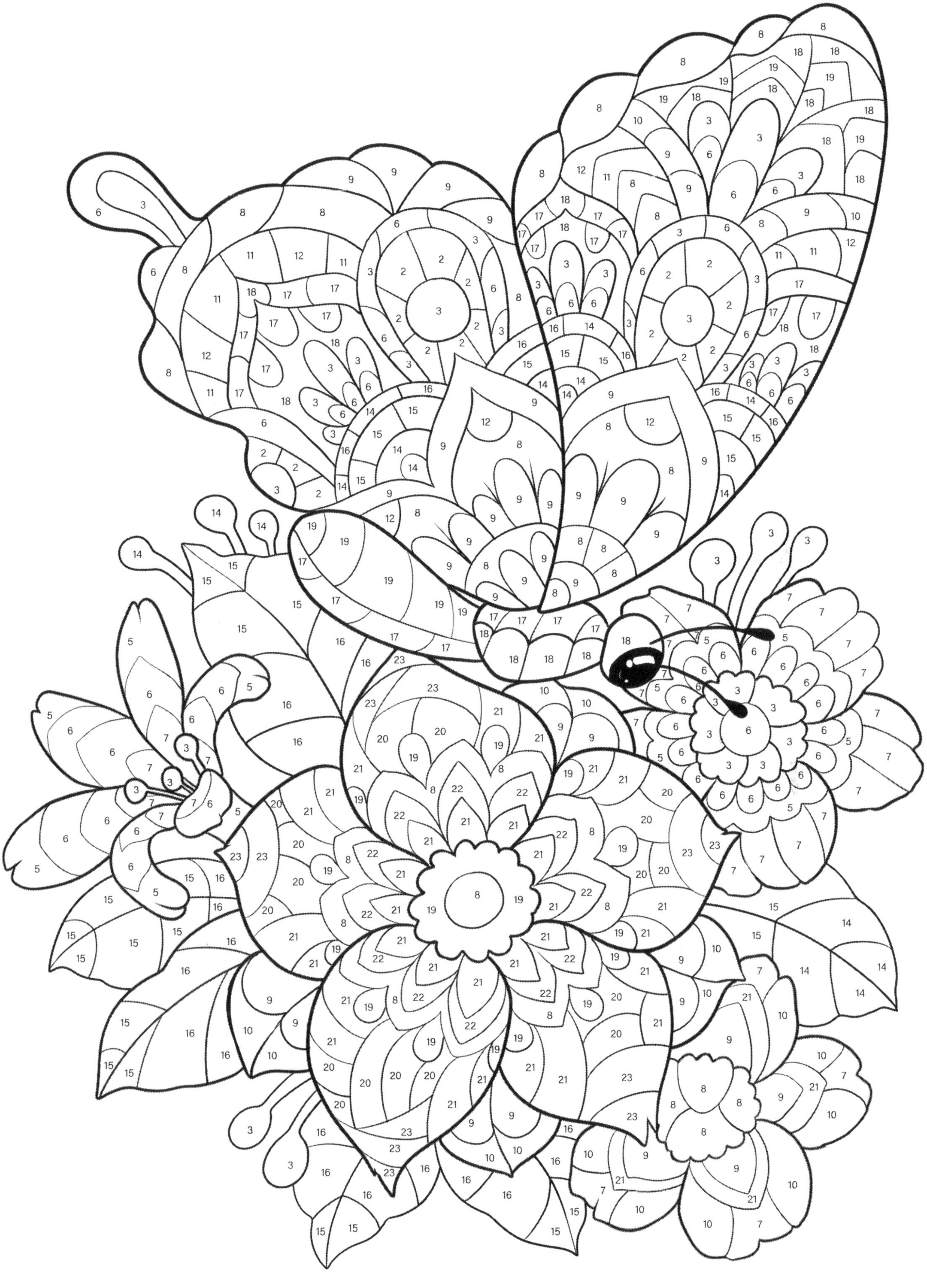

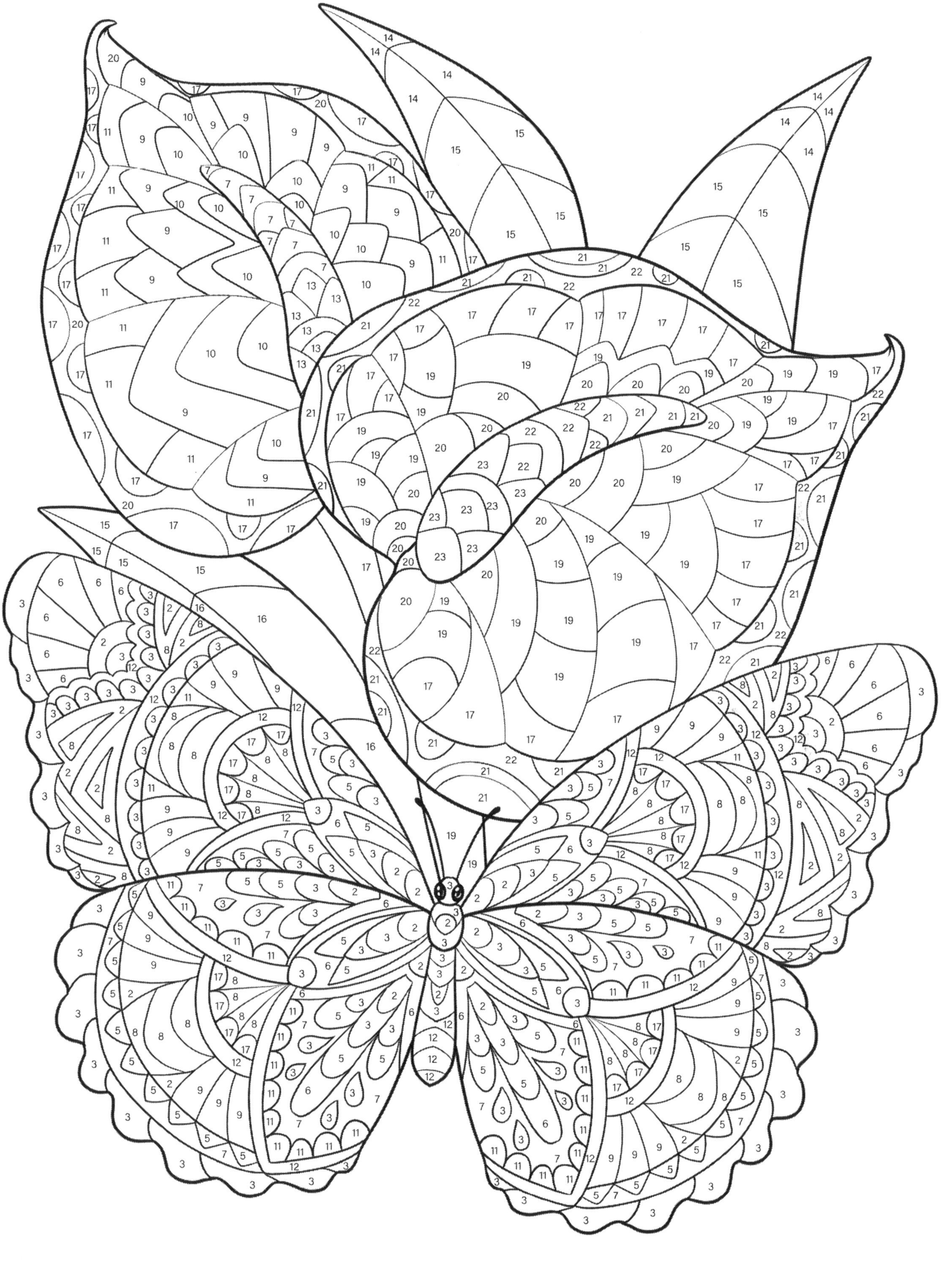

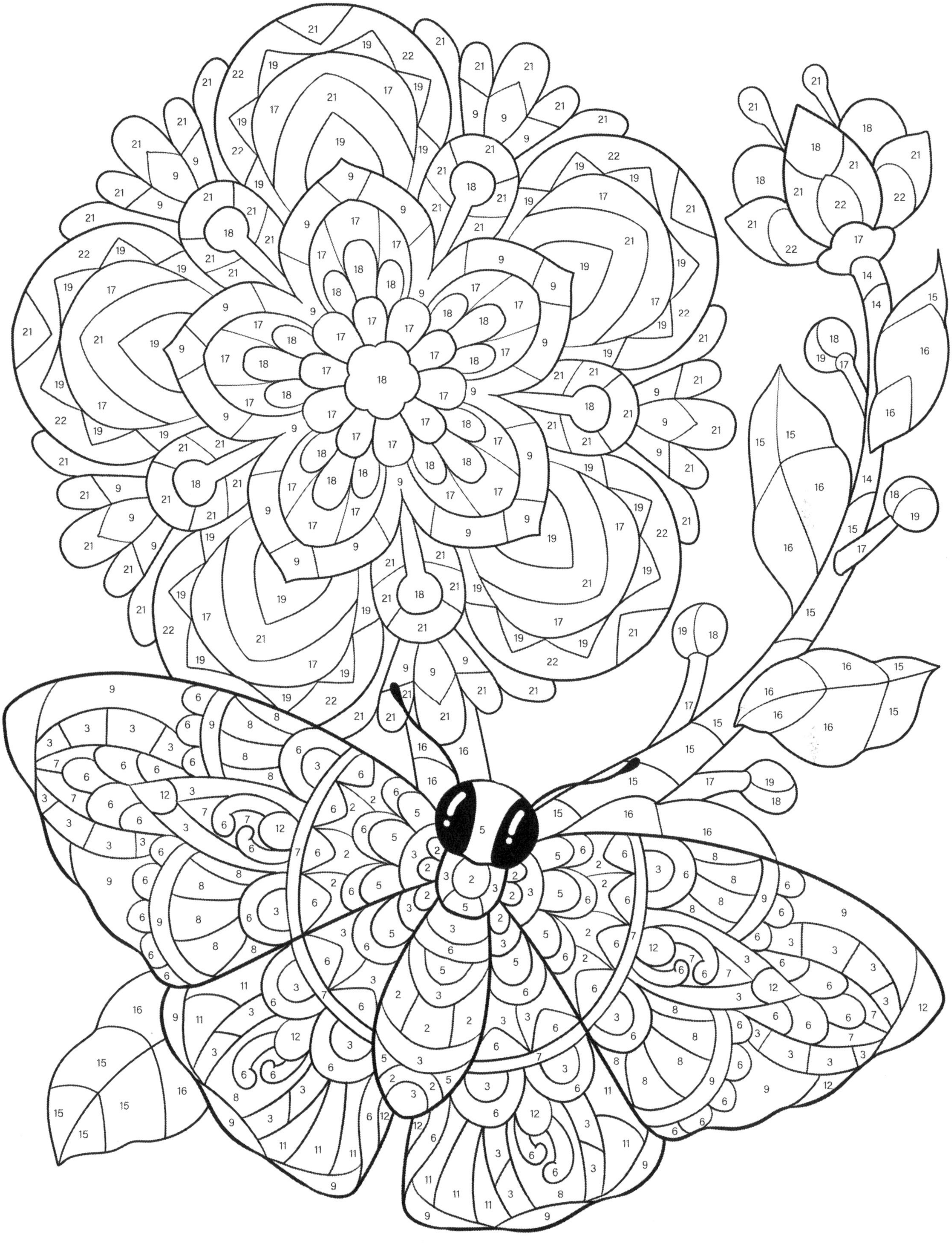

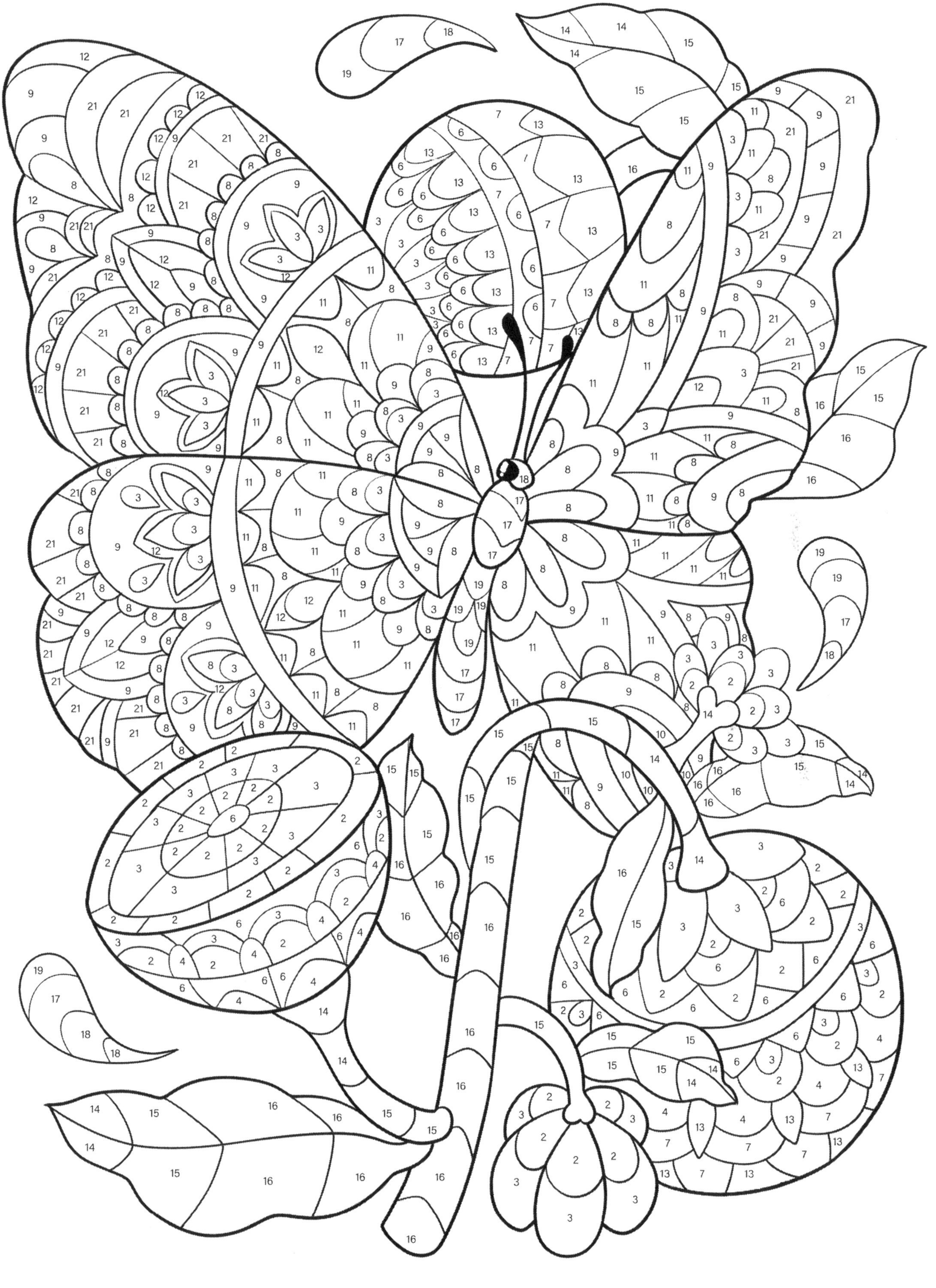